TULIP'S JOURNEY

BRANDY SPRATTLING

Illustrated by Maggui Ledbetter

Tulip's Journey
Text copyright © 2020 by Brandy Sprattling
Illustrations copyright © 2020 by Maggui Ledbetter

All rights reserved. This book or any portion thereof
may not be reproduced or used in any manner whatsoever
without the express written permission of the publisher
except for the use of brief quotations in a book review.

For inquiries, contact:
mrssprattlingscreativeworks@gmail.com

Printed in the United States of America

Editing: Sue Peterson
Illustrations: Maggui Ledbetter
Book Design: Carla Green, Clarity Designworks

ISBN: 978-1-7355874-0-0

To God who loves me, saved me, and has blessed me so much
and who is the true author of this book.

To my husband, Karl, who believed in me before I believed in myself.

To my three beautiful children: Mercedes, Carlos, and Karly,
who gave me the motivation to pursue my dreams.

To all the amazing children I have ever had the pleasure of teaching
who made me a better teacher in every way.

When Tulip was a little bulb, she had many hopes and dreams that were unusual for tulips.

Each day, as the sun came up, she tried to break through the hard, rocky surface. But, each day, something seemed to stop her.

First, there was not enough rain to soften the dirt so she could not get through.

Then, there were too many pebbles in her way.

But Tulip knew she was made for greatness
because of the dreams she held in her heart.
So, each day, she continued to hope.

One day, after a long rain, the ground became soft. The pebbles shifted, and Tulip saw sunlight peeking through the darkness.

As she stretched toward the light,
she heard footsteps above.

Suddenly, someone stepped on her surface
packing the dirt down again and taking away the light.

But, Tulip knew she was made for greatness because of the dreams she held in her heart, so Tulip said to herself, "I am not giving up."

Then, one day, after another long rain,
the pebbles shifted again. Tulip saw the sunlight
peeking through the darkness once more.

This time, as Tulip s-t-r-e-t-c-h-e-d for the light, she was a little bit taller and stronger and with all her might she finally broke through!

It felt magnificent! Tulip's heart opened from the warmth of the sun. As it did, her petals exploded with the most vibrant pink color the world had ever seen. "I am free!" Tulip exclaimed.

Just then, Tulip remembered the dreams she held in her heart,
and it beat wildly with excitement as she imagined
all she would be and all she would do.

Suddenly, Tulip heard a loud noise and the earth began to shake. She looked around to see a large tractor rumbling toward her.

As it moved closer, it dug up the earth destroying the stillness of her home.

Tulip looked in every direction and hoped for a miracle to save her as the dirt flew everywhere. But, even with the tractor coming full speed, Tulip knew she was made for greatness because of the dreams she held in her heart so she continued to hope as the loud machine headed straight for her.

Tulip put her head down to brace for impact and as she did, the big, loud machine just stopped.

A man jumped out of the machine and ran over to Tulip. He bent down and lifted her head. "Oh, Tulip," he said. "Why is your head bent down and why are you so scared? Do you not know that I planted you here long ago and put all your hopes and dreams in your heart? I was just waiting for you to realize your strength and push through the darkness."

Tulip's heart smiled as she realized the farmer loved her
and was always close by, waiting for the day
when she would reach for the sunlight.

The farmer unearthed Tulip and placed her securely in a pot. "Come on," he said. "Let's go home where every one of your dreams will come true."

The End

About the Author

Brandy Sprattling is a wife, mother of three, and a teacher. Prior to teaching, she worked as an estate planning paralegal for 17 years. After teaching Sunday School for many years, she decided to finish her education and become an elementary school teacher. She currently teaches in the Central Valley of California. She holds a teaching credential in elementary education, a teaching credential in English (K-12), and is eligible for an Administrative Service credential. Brandy graduated *summa cum laude* from Fresno Pacific University where she earned her bachelor's degree in Liberal Arts. She is currently earning a master's degree in Curriculum and Instruction from Grand Canyon University. She has always had a love for writing and understands how reading and writing can be used to teach valuable social-emotional lessons to children and adults. It is her desire to inspire children through her writing to believe in themselves and pursue their dreams.

About the Illustrator

Maggui Ledbetter graduated from CSU Fresno with a bachelor's degree and a teaching credential. After teaching for Los Banos Unified School District for thirty years, Maggui retired and now spends her days painting at home in her art studio. She enjoys painting with watercolors and acrylics and has a passion for using art to express the farmer's struggles with water shortages and politics and their love of farming. Maggui has illustrated for books such as *How Far is Heaven*, *Blanket of Miracles*, and her own authored book entitled *The Pink Can Notes*. Maggui looks forward to more years of writing and painting.

CPSIA information can be obtained at www.ICGtesting.com
Printed in the USA
LVIW010842131020
668670LV00012B/790